SUGAR-PAPER BLUE

Sugar-Paper Blue

RUTH FAINLIGHT

BLOODAXE BOOKS

ISBN: 1 85224 419 4

First published 1997 by
Bloodaxe Books Ltd,
P.O. Box 1SN,
Newcastle upon Tyne NE99 1SN.

Bloodaxe Books Ltd acknowledges
the financial assistance of Northern Arts.

Cover printing by J. Thomson Colour Printers Ltd, Glasgow.

Printed in Great Britain by
Cromwell Press Ltd, Broughton Gifford, Melksham, Wiltshire.

for Michèle Duclos

Acknowledgements

Acknowledgements are due to the editors of the following publications in which these poems, sometimes in different forms, first appeared: *Agenda*, *Columbia* (USA), *Hudson Review* (USA), *Jerusalem Report* (Israel), *The Jewish Quarterly*, *London Review of Books*, *The New Yorker* (USA), *Obsessed with Pipework*, *Oxford Quarterly Review*, *PN Review*, *Poetry London Newsletter*, *Poetry Review*, *The Rialto*, *Southern Review* (USA), *Thirteenth Moon* (USA), *Times Literary Supplement*, *Threepenny Review* (USA), *Thumbscrew*; to *Éditions de l'Eau* (France) for the volume *Pomegranate*, comprising the poem and six mezzotints by Judith Rothchild; and to the *New Seizin Press*, Deya, Mallorca.

Contents

I

Agua de Colonia

The sharp smell of cheap eau-de-cologne,
agua de colonia, will call it back:
every aspect of the lonely summer
in that other era, when I was young.

Watered pavements of narrow streets between
old buildings. Dim high-ceilinged cafés blue
with smoke from yellow-papered cigarettes.
The almost neutral taste of almond *horchata*
in a tall glass beaded with moisture. I pressed
my wrists against its sides to cool my blood.

Molten sunlight through the shutter slats
corrodes the floor-tiles' lozenges and arabesques.
Insomnia under a mosquito net.
My scent. My languor. My formal clothing.

The Bowl

*crescent (of
shape
liquid?)*

She was like a bowl filled with liquid
pushing against the meniscus, up
to the brim, waiting
                    for something
to tip it over, let all it holds
flow freely,
            for someone who knows
that however rich and rare, unless
spilled out its contents must stagnate
decay and parch.
                    But the bowl sits so
well balanced, as if nothing less than
a cyclone could budge it,
                        and the other
grows doubtful, while the weather stubbornly
stays in the doldrums, unbearably calm...

Pomegranate

Its twisted stem is rough as hessian twine,
its skin taut as the head of a drum,
its angled form an ancient box streaked by
metallic lustres green and red and bronze.
The seeds inside are chunks of ruby crystal
that grit between my teeth like broken glass
and melt like lumps of sweetened ice, the mesh
of pith that holds them, jewellers' chamois wrapped
around a garnet necklace, or worn suede gloves.

*

Two pomegranates, one larger, one smaller
grown from the same stem, close to each other
like two sisters,
mother and daughter.

It took several tries to get them down
from the highest part of the tree –
the long-handled fruit-picker just not reaching
or pushing the branch further away.

Proud of their orchard, their rabbits and chickens,
Luisa and Catalina had already gathered a cluster
of green lemons and the first ripe clementines:
lemons, clementines and pomegranates
I brought back to London.

Persephone and Pluto and Demeter
were names unknown to the sisters
(so many teaching stories
for outrage, grief and compromise),
but they told me of their mother's death
and gave me pomegranates, saying,
'If you eat one, we shall meet again.'

*

No one knew where it was, when I tried to find their street.
'Somewhere up there?'
　　　　　　　'Near the market?'
　　　　　　　　　　　　'Sounds familiar'.
Even the townhall guard wasn't sure.
I wondered, had it been re-named?
couldn't understand
how people who lived in such a small place
didn't know their neighbourhood geography.
But I had gone so often to that house
twenty-five and thirty years before,
with lengths of cloth, for tryings-on and final fittings.
(I still wear clothes they made.)

Ten years sooner,
might someone else have recognised me?
In cafés and shops, market and square,
the welcomes imagined – unformulated
triumphs and pleasures – did not happen.
The irrelevance of disillusion.
But I wanted to see Luisa. That much I knew.

Starting again, I let instinct guide me
down narrow streets past wooden doors
half-open onto fern-cool courtyards.
I felt a tightening in my chest, then,
(false first impression) an old woman,
black-clothed, bent over, rounded the corner.
It happened so quickly. In less
than a moment. Absolute recognition.
I heard my own voice: 'Luisa? Is it Luisa?'
The same soft cheeks, gone slacker, creased
and those uncertain, affectionate eyes peered
through the decades. 'Señora! Is it really you?'

　　　　　　　*

Luisa, who used to be wary, seemed skittish,
effusive – but fragile. I was nervous.
I didn't want to distress or exhaust her.
Catalina, the simpler, still smiled eagerly.
Withered convent girls
who today must be aged about sixty.

No brothers, no other sisters, no nephews or nieces.
Luisa nodded toward garden and livestock.
'No one to help now, or live here after –
we'll have to decide what to do.'

My hand clutched with playground urgency,
I was hurried to the rabbit hutch.
'Eleven babies, and her first time!'
She lifted one to show me.
A tender, work-stained finger
stroked the velvet squirmer.
From the terrace, Luisa watched.

Catalina never learned about Persephone,
but had other knowledge just as ancient –
would not take a doe to the buck
at the lunar waning.
Low-angled afternoon sun slanted dusty rays
through fruit and leaves of the orange trees,
burnished them to Fabergé toys
or an emperor's grave-goods,
and magnified her meagre frame
clothed in a not-too-clean housedress
to the dimensions of a mother goddess
as she explained how every sort
of seed grows better and stronger
if planted under a waxing moon.
'Everyone knows it,' she said, matter-of-fact.

*

Turning off the coast road
from olive down through orange groves,
first sight of the valley –
　　　morning haze, encircling mountains:
　　　that exact line against the sky
　　　prototype for every horizon
　　　etched on my mind's eye
　　　annealed into my memory
　　　in another age, an endless time…

Driving away at sunset,
as the car climbed loops and bends
I noticed how the road was widened;
looking back, saw new apartment blocks
and houses; behind Luisa's orchard
the dusty squalor of a building site.

That particular gesture remained unaltered:
the way her head would slant to one shoulder
and a hand deprecatingly fall
while she gently complained
of the cousin who had sold his garden.

*

Empty pomegranate husks discarded
when I split the fruit to suck its juices
strewn across my table
like corroded armour, tarnished goblets
or the casing of an archaic bomb
burnt and rusted by earth's ardent acids,
only now exhumed.

*

Whatever stayed forgotten,
memory, more cunning
than the finest tailor
had stitched decades and moments
truth and confusion
unrecovered facts
pious error
into a seamless garment.

Was I as unchanged (the same
friendly foreigner) to Luisa
and her sister (my two chosen
innocents) as they were for me?
Stranger yet closer.
Until we meet in Pluto's realm
to share our pomegranate seeds
I shall not know.

The Lizard

A lizard's agile scuttle
to clear their speeding car;

then her gesture, later, back home,
urgently crumpling a letter

into her pocket, insisting
no mail had come, none at all.

Linked determinations
to save something vital:

its life, for the lizard – for her,
the freedom to enjoy

anything on offer,
whatever else got spoiled.

*

The lizard's action was focussed,
total, its dull green body

and legs splayed wide were fixed
on survival. She was also.

Yet her manner seemed more
ambiguous, not quite

guilty; annoyed would be
a better word, he thought.

A shame he's so observant –
he wonders just what's worth

this much anguish. (Though
she veered to avoid the lizard.)

The Same

The same wound you made
now you want to cure –
yet when the torn and bloody
tissues, soothed, begin to mend
you tear the scarf-skin off once more.

The same dagger, thrust
into my flesh, you use
to trim new bandages –
then rip away the half-formed scar.
And healing hurts the most of all.

The same gentle words
and acts – or cruel, cruel.
Which is worse to bear?
The tape reverses, but still spools
the same tales of love and war.

The Old Typewriter

Every time the letter 'O'
was struck on the old typewriter
you lent me last summer,
it punched a hole in the paper.

I wondered what pattern of lace
the punctured page might weave
on a jaquard loom, what tune
play out from a pianola,

and if, when held to a lamp or
window it would read in code;
whether the poems I typed
last summer sent another
message, contradicting
what I thought I wrote.

Friends' Photos

We all looked like goddesses
and gods, glowing and smooth, sheathed
from head to foot by a golden essence
that glistened and refracted its aura
of power – the wonderful ichor called youth.

We moved as easily as dolphins
surging out of the ocean, cleaving
massed tons of transparent water
streaming away in swathes of bubbling
silver like the plasm of life.

Still potent from those black and white
photos, the palpable electric
charge between us, like the negative
and positive poles of a battery,
or the fingers of Adam and God.

We were beautiful, without exception.
I could hardly bear to look at those
old albums, to see the lost glamour
we never noticed when we were
first together – when we were young.

Young Men

Young men disturb me as they never used to –
a sharply physical disturbance, with full
awareness that stiff joints and slack flesh
no longer could perform what I imagine;
mind and body
                              moving further apart.

I feel a tenderness and sympathy
for old body, that poor donkey, most
burdens too heavy now, though once little
seemed beyond it; ruefully acknowledge
how only rage and lust
                              augment with time.

Whether mind becomes more tolerant
to repetition of the same absurdities,
nothing learned, is a moot point.
But those young men – ought I to want
the day ever to come
                              when they don't disturb?

Maenad

Once upon a time
I ranged the mountains
with the rest, the best, arms
raised high, head thrown back,
bright brief breast bare, etc,
etc. They said I looked
as if I had danced off the side
of an Attic vase. My legs
were strong. My nails were sharp.
My laugh was wild.

What happens next, after
frenzy and consummation,
after stumbling home to swab
away the blood, pick
dark hairs from teeth and tongue,
vomit gobbets of fat and skin?
Time works the changes:
maenad – matron – crone – (who
still remembers how it felt;
everything).

Silly

Age also brings its silliness.
I watch two white-haired sisters
in my train compartment

features blurred and faded
worked over by the seasons
as dolls forgotten in the garden

who once were stern brunettes –
daughters, wives, mistresses
a suburb's heartbreakers –

flirting with the ticket-collector
and simpering for approval
as I used to – Daddy's little darling.

Whatever

This urgent impatience comes with getting older.
I'm sure I once was able to hold out longer,
psce my pleasures and accept postponement.
These days though, I crave them instant, constant.

I thought it was supposed to slow by now.
But this fear of being about to scream or cry,
goad someone dear into a fateful quarrel
by pointless vicious words, or gulp down a tumbler
of vodka, doesn't conform to the model
I'd hoped was possible: self-control.

I want events to be closer together,
things to keep happening, one after another,
like the dizzying progression of yellow-painted
warning chevrons on the oil-stained macadam or
the fluttering blur of pennants and trees in the wind
at the auto-route's verge; as if perpetual change
and movement against whatever background – that
unaltering horizon – were my sole protection.

Eyeliner

How long ago? it's hard to remember –
this time of early evening, late
September, days shortening, the same
traffic sounds – I'd be making up,
painting a careful line under
each eye, smudging the upper lid,
getting ready...

One could almost say, nothing has
changed: the same excitement, the same
style come round again – except
that I was starting then; now I've
learned that though the traffic and
the parties carry on, there
will be other hands, harsh or
kind, to get me ready, under-
line and darken my eyes before
they close them.

Milky Way

Under the spout of the shower,
lifting an arm to soap the armpit –
recurrent gestures
               that open onto
a flickering continuum,
like a zoetrope...
             The girl in Virginia
who lay on her back in the bathtub
to let the water needle her body
deliciously and the woman
in England, meditatively washing,
enacting the same movements...
                    One
remembers, the other puzzles why
she feels the moment returning,
streaming before – behind –
                circling
as water spirals, clockwise, counter
clockwise – as a cloud
of dust and gas coagulates
into a galaxy...
             While the shower
patterns her body, scalp to footsole,
with a pelt of irridescent foam
like a map of the Milky Way.

Chained Angel

Since I stood it outside my front door,
this almost life-sized wooden figure,
I've questioned visitors on their opinion
of my angel's gender – whether it more resembles
a Duccio virgin or Uccello warrior.
The angel's attribute: a branch of palm,
its dress: a simple robe, and hair curled
to the shoulder, are not specific to either.

At first you think it's there to guard my door.
Then you notice a length of chain attached
between statue and floor – how else to guard
my captive, so ambiguous and helpless,
whose plumy wings are shackled, pinioned,
who cannot protect me nor itself from harm?
It has another purpose. I fear my angel
soon will utter what I do not want to hear.

II

The Mercury Vapour Moth Trap

I

He always put it out before dusk:
some moths are crepuscular.
Metres of electric cable,
like power lines for a pop-concert,
were strung between the trees
to the furthest part of the garden, to keep
the light as far away as possible:
white light and ultra-violet light
from a lurid, incandescent bulb
whose central purple pulse and throb
was not to be looked at;
(u.v. is the primary attractant).

II

How to describe a mercury vapour moth trap?
Imagine a black plastic drum
with the circumference of a tractor tyre,
and a funnel shaped baffle –
an entomological lobster-pot –
channelling down to empty egg boxes
like the grey cells of a brain cross-section
for the moths to roost on.
He said they found it comforting.

III

That summer
my schoolboy son
commandeered a shed
normally used for storing tools or wood.
Every morning
from the kitchen window
I watched him (he had grown that year
to almost the size of a man)
stumble into the yard
clutching the dew and grass-smeared object
high against his chest,
twist half-around to get a hand
near enough to press down the latch,
then loop back a foot to close the door.

IV

Some days there were ten; others, hundreds.
If he moved gently, he proudly told me,
not more than a quarter flew up.
He would log them all in his notebook,
numbers and species,
ease anything special
carefully into the killing bottle,
then carry the trap to the brambles
at the end of the orchard
and watch the swarm disperse
into the bushes and long grass,
under every leaf and stalk.
He could stand there and muse for hours.

V

Once only I ventured into his realm –
a dim space thick with layers of movement
like the swaying of dirt-stiffened curtains
in a half-demolished house:
last year's spiderwebs and coaldust,
this day's filaments, antennae, scales;
confusing and, yes, I'm sure I heard a sound –
the beat of panicking wings,
an ultra-sonic wail of distress;
and my own shriek: shocking, immediate,
as the fulvous dusty mass
like a drench of slush from a cornering car
flapped against my face.
Until evening I snorted and spat
fragments, the bitter smell and taste
from nostrils and mouth.

VI

Specimen boxes, carried
since then from loft to loft.
Rusted pins and faded wings.
An excellent collection of moths.

Hendon Central

Driving north past Hendon Central parade –
which doesn't look much changed – I have a flashback
to the cotton fabric: loose weave, pale green, white
floral print, of my first-year summer uniform.
(My parents sent me to the local private school.)

Dressed in the same quaint gear, class-mates and I
would stop to look each way (good children!)
before risking what was not yet a dangerous
junction where two four-lane main roads meet
but a suburban crossroad, and race to the sweetshop.

Its small-paned window level with the pavement,
dark steps down to the narrow space between counter and
shelves jammed with stock, even then seemed outdated,
a story-book illustration. My favourites were
the liquorice straps rolled round sugared almonds –

though when I had to choose (and could resist
the candy-lure) I'd use my pocket-money –
coins as blackened as if long buried,
pale images and letters barely legible –
for packets of Japanese paper flowers.

In a plain jar of clear water, scalloped
scraps and folded strips of coloured paper
would soften, open, spread, miraculously,
into the abstract forms of leaves – petals –
blossoms – and air bubbles cling like diamonds

to the creaking, glittering branches of the midnight
forest in *The Twelve Dancing Princesses* when
the gardener's boy followed the one he loved.
The cunning of it! I longed to know what really
happened – how everything was done.

Nature

'It's natural,' my mother would say,
as though the word had power to justify
and was the highest praise.
'Natural!' I scoffed. 'Like a cancer eating up someone.
Like war and death and pain.'

Nature meant flowers and babies
to her, not a slaughterer but a shepherdess.
She wouldn't have been out of place
at the Petit Trianon, with Marie Antoinette.
Remembering her panic-struck face

when I protested against
such Panglossian blindness to the indifference
of Nature, God, Fate –
whatever one called it (I was so infantile) –
still makes me itch with shame.

A girl of my age
should have known better, stopped tormenting her mother.
But when she went on about Nature
I refused to listen. She admitted nothing.
Not even gas chambers.

Horns

(This refers to the old belief that, as in
Michelangelo's 'Moses', Jews are horned.)

Before my walk
I went to look
at the trusting calves,
their onyx eyes.
Instead, I saw,
livid, red,
between whorled hairs
white and black,
raw shallow wounds
and bloody clots
where budding horns
had been cauterised.

Then full recall –
the school playground:
its asphalt surface
gritty, harsh,
to knees and hands
of the one downed
by a press of children
daring each other
to push thick fingers
through springy curls
above her temples
and find the horns.

Evacuee

The secret of life had some connection then
to the ivory sprout of a flat pale bean –
pointed tip and crumpled seed-leaves straining
up between a moistened wad of cotton
wool and the curved shine of a glass jar
in the airless classroom where our teacher
prosed on nature's wonders. The glow it shed.

Or the hot throb of a bird in my hand –
a fledgling, fallen from its nest, rescued
from the crater of a cowpat; the shock
of its raucous protest, its open
amber beak and pulsing throat bright
as crocus petals; the globule of dung
that slid like an egg onto my unnerved palm.

Or the long wicks of white pith packed inside
the clumped hard green stems of rushes I'd split
with the nail of my thumb – which pricked my legs
as I ran – and the thick runnel of blood
from my knee the day I tripped, reading a book,
not looking where I was going. The scar,
tattooed by coaldust, which marks it still.

Dinah *(Genesis 34)*

'High-spirited and martial men among all nations and throughout history have often yielded to blind cruelty when dealing with an outrage of this nature.'

(note to Genesis 34.31, SONCINO: *Pentateuch & Haftorahs*)

Holding up my hands in warning,
I want to call, 'No! No! Don't do it!',
to Shechem and Dinah, to Simeon and Levi,
but most of all, to every able-bodied male
of Hamor's tribe. 'Don't consent, it's a trap.'

Swollen tender flesh:
Shechem's, aching with lust and love
(he told his father, 'Get me this damsel to wife',
he 'spoke comfortingly unto the damsel');
Dinah's broken maidenhead;
Hamor's guards, weakened by pain,
three days after circumcision.

That was the moment chosen to destroy them,
spoil the city, take their flocks and herds,
enslave their wives and little ones, while
Dinah's brothers led her back to Jacob's tents,
ancient honour satisfied.

Jacob chided his sons, fearful
that Canaanites and Perizzites
would now combine against him.
Not until he lay dying
did he curse them for that wild vengeance.
What Dinah thought of Shechem's death
is never mentioned.

'No, no, don't do it!',
I want to call out,
palms upward, heart pounding.
'Choose another future!'
But it's always too late or too soon.
So much still must happen.
The story has just begun.

Fatima

Fatima put down the broom
to lift the blue-eyed boy
(who crowed with joy) from his cot
with strong dark hands and arms,
to show him the bright blue sky,
the pine-coned branch that over-
hung the terrace, boats
on the glittering sea. Her smile
was broad, yet poignant.
'So blond and fat! So red and white!'
Her gold tooth gleamed. 'Little
turnip! I'll gobble you up.'

Fatima sat in the playground
at Kensington Gardens
watching the foreign children.
She wanted to try it all:
slide, roundabout and swings,
had never dreamt such toys
existed, when she was small.
But everything was different
here – like the slant-eyed man
with yellow skin, who followed
one afternoon, as she pushed
the pram, to see where she lived.

Fatima locked in a room:
the first months of marriage
for a frightened thirteen-year-old.
After the ceremony, as
was customary, her husband
only arrived for meals;
ate, smoked, pulled her onto
the bed, then disappeared.
For hours she would look
at the patterns of flaking paint
on the lime-washed wall and
the houses opposite.

A group of women used to
sit on that roof and henna
each others' hair. She tried
to catch their words. It was worst if
they laughed. She imagined their names,
what their children were called, but
no one came except the man
and his mother, until the midwife
they brought when the pains began.
Two weeks later the fever
broke and she heard them say
the baby, a boy, was dead.

Fatima had three daughters.
When too much *kif* killed her husband,
she sent them to her sister's
village and their throng of cousins.
Whatever hurt, she ignored or
forgot – a trusted servant
and nursemaid now in other women's
families. The best were *Nasrani*.
One Madame took her to London.
(The little turnip had cried
and screamed and clung.) Some days
she knew he was her son.

Two Pictures by Judith Rothchild

1 *Three Jars*

Tall jars, red earthenware vessels
held together in a network of pale mastic,
swirls of green and yellow glaze
dribbled down from the incised double lip
to the high-waisted swell of the fullest part,
  handles like the small ears of archaic
  Cycladic crop-haired athletes' statues,

are standing against a grainy wall
  (which could have been built by Cyclops),
  each lichen-blotch and roughness
  in the pitted cemented surface softened
  by centuries of sun and storm;
whose blunted edge presses into the sky
(harsh blue with a few high strato-
cumulus clouds) the same firm line
as the mountains behind, like another horizon:
an almost primeval landscape
of small peaks, threatening to erupt,

  as if these jars had been brought
  from the cindered slopes of Santorin
  to the side of a scarlet lake
  at the foot of the Massif.

II *Queen of the Nile*

Black Sarah, the gypsies' Virgin,
Queen of the Nile and
the three Marys' servant,

With Virgin Mary, Mary her sister
and Mary Magdalen, after the crucifixion,
was put in a boat lacking sails and rudder

but which found miraculous harbour
under the cliffs of Les Baux, when
storms drove them far inshore.

Now, an agapanthus lily,
the blue, African, 'Queen of the Nile',
flowers on a Languedoc terrace

as if Sarah, worshipped as a saint
from Sete to Agde to Aigues Mortes,
turns proud dark eyes toward

the long view down the littoral,
where her tomb is guarded, all night through,
by fishermen and wanderers.

Vendange

(for Mark Lintott)

The hollow thud as a bunch of grapes,
bloomed like new-dug minerals
in every shade of grey from dark
to pale – jade, bloodstone,
malachite – lands in the bucket,
the rustle of wind through leaves
already crimson and purple-stained.

Every vine is different:
this one's clusters glossy,
heavy and easy to cut. On that,
each stem is trapped, twisted
around another, and must be clipped
in sections; the centre is rotten,
powdery, mildewed and black.

Plunging your hands into some
you feel like a midwife at a difficult
birth, a butcher doing
a disembowelment. You touch
the Bacchic source. With the best
you become a châtelaine
culling her orchid house.

Dry and harsh as wire,
teasels and burrs – tenacious
little hooks like centipede
claws, almost impossible
to detach – infiltrate.
Whatever you wear for the job
will be ruined, or chafe for weeks.

Vendangers' hands are filthy,
varnished with pulp and juice and earth,
stained in every pore and crease.
When I saw what went into the vat,
I thought I'd never drink
another glass. But soon, I'm sure,
this bottle will be empty.

Ancient Egyptian Couples

Ancient Egyptian couples
standing or seated side by side.
Plaited wigs and pleated robes
breastplates and bracelets patterned
with lotus and papyrus buds
in wood, stone, plaster,
meticulously worked and incised.

Signifying separate realms,
his skin is painted
earth red, hers gleams soft
and golden as the sky.

Sometimes, the wife has placed a hand
upon her husband's shoulder.
They stare at us, not at each other,
from enormous kohl-rimmed eyes.

That surge of affection
across millennia, like
the sudden return of desire
which haloes the head, the whole
body, of the one confirmed
again as beloved, brings them
close as you and I.

Woodman

You cut some branches, also a bough
from the tree outside my room
to widen the view and let
me see as far as the vineyards,
but a stiff and sullen mood
would not allow one word
of thanks or pleasure.

Something is wrong with my eyes –
they only recognise the past,
with my heart – it only beats
nostalgia or remorse,
with my mind – which cannot learn
until too late, too late,
only values what is lost.

Afterwards, I could look
across the vines to the lone tree
not quite at the top of the hill
and the square Saracen tower
the village doctor was rebuilding –
none of which had been visible
before you played the woodman.

Woodman, will you trim the lilac,
the hawthorn and the hazel
in another garden,
reveal the line of hills
behind another house? Now
I know how little time is left
to prove I'm grateful.

III

The Corset Lady

How long is it since I noticed one of those discreet corsetry shops on a leafy side street off the main boulevards, small show-window lined with dull-toned grosgrain drapes against which the sole identifying object on display was the plaster figure, half or quarter life-sized, of a female torso topped by a modestly pretty head and face whose demure vacuous gaze evaded every admirer? The surprisingly full and shapely body would be clasped by an elaborate girdle: boned, hooked, bound and strapped – all the skills of corsetière-proprietor exhibited like a sampler stitched by an 18th century girl as evidence of her skill, and the truncated lower parts veiled by a frill of faded écru lace. How delightful to have a little lady like that at home, for my very own. Preferably alive.

My mother would laugh indulgently as I elaborated the fantasy. But later, older, arm in arm with some uncertain young suitor, if I stopped entranced before such an illuminated display, I sensed a certain uneasiness, even alarm, to hear this wish expressed.

By the time I came to appreciate their miniature allure, these figures were anachronisms. Their worn appearance testified that no replacements existed. Chips and knocks inflicted while being moved in and out of the window for trappings to be adjusted or changed, revealed dead white (or crumbling, porous, dirty) plaster under the painted surface. Through the slow effects of time and dust, their painted features darkened into a curdled puce and mottled ochre that evoked the complexions of those plaster heads with antique coiffures and missing noses – like saints in post-Reformation churches – which still survived in occasional hair-dressing salons of the outlying suburbs, or the powdered faces of their increasingly short-winded clientele.

Sometimes, between glowing globes of green and purple liquids in shabby pharmacies, I would sight the plaster figure of a man – proportions similar to those of the corset lady, but usually with all limbs and parts intact – garlanded by bandages, trusses, and splints. The two of them seemed to form a pair: a devoted couple maimed and cruelly separated by the exigencies of survival. But I do not recall any urge to reunite them, nor ever wanting to take the little man home with me.

Hand Shoes

She is a honey-skinned hazel-blonde, faint laughter lines radiating from sleepy, witty eyes, and dimples at each side of full unpainted lips compressed as if about to smile – a mouth around which, in certain lights, through the mesh of her veil, pale down glistens: the woman wearing fine tanned leather 'hand-shoes', (or gloves, as English terms them). They are chestnut coloured and slightly stained at the palm by her moist, perfumed skin, with elaborately stitched gussets between each finger and flaring over the wrist. *Der Handschuhe.* She is walking on her feet, in polished high-heeled boots, and not on her hands, towards the city's best café to meet her Hussar and drink a cup of coffee. I half expect her to stretch and arch that supple spine, raise to the sky then lower to the ground tight-sleeved, stiff-elbowed arms, slowly roll back her head, and paw the earth as if those small shod hands were hooves and she the mate of a centaur.

The Tooth Fairy

She liked watching him at work – the concentrated expression, the clean-shaved skin, every pore visible as if under a magnifying glass, the well-trimmed nails and immaculate tunic and smoothly pelted arms. She registered his scrupulous odourlessness, the trimmed nostrils and perfectly maintained teeth. And there were more intimate aspects of contact: the faint but definite pleasure as he slid a finger along her gums and the responding desire to bite or lick it, or those times when, struggling to extract the recalcitrant shards of a shattered root, his body cantilevered across hers as if they were wrestling or making love.

Her brother loved to touch her teeth when they were children, which had irritated and disturbed her. She remembered his avid expression, and unsuccessful attempts to evade his hands. 'Of course you smash your own teeth,' a friend commented. 'There's nothing else you can let yourself smash!' She wasn't aware of anything unusual about her bite. Sexual pleasure makes the teeth melt. In the extreme of sexual spasm, not only hands and feet but even teeth seemed to dissolve into pulpy plasm, like the primal stuff of a half-term embryo, or the curdled liquid inside a chrysallis where an insect metamorphosed to its final state. There were dreams in which every tooth in her head fell onto the ground.

Conflicting odours of mouthwash, impression plaster, amalgam and abrasive; the stink of charred bone and infected tissue and their taste in her mouth; the high-pitched whine and whirr of drill or aspirator; the focused beam of the chair lamp and the glare and glitter of overhead neon reflected from smooth white surfaces and the line-up of probes, mirrors and instruments whose name she had never learned; the fine spray of water which cooled the drill and beaded her face; the flutter and nausea as the anaesthetic hit; the ache in her back; the sometimes barely tolerable restlessness and tension – or a flaccid languor compounded of discomfort, boredom, and fear; and those rare occasions when a part of herself floated towards the ceiling to observe benignly what was being done to the body which normally contained it: such were the pains and pleasures of their meetings.

In a small painted box on her dressing-table lay two recently extracted molars. There had been a certain surprise and even (she wondered) disgust at the request for these bloody souvenirs as soon as she was able to speak again, but they were wrapped in cotton wool and put into an envelope for her to take home. The fanglike curve of their roots and rough surface to which a faint meaty residue of gum tissue still clung, and the smooth enamel with its golden inlay of filling, made them resemble shamanic amulets, and for a time she thought of wearing them on a chain around her neck, to mark her thralldom to the tooth fairy.

Bruises

At first my face looked smeared
with dust or earth or soot, like
bread when it starts to go mouldy.
Then slate-blue brightened to purple
and a curdled green tinge
flushed up like the underpainting
on a Byzantine ikon
or a ghostly Duccio Virgin.

After the swelling's gone,
the bruises faded, I certainly
hope there won't be another
occasion – though watching the changes
(there must be a fixed sequence:
something to do with rates of decay
of bloodclots or protein?)
was interesting.

Pain

The track of an electric
storm sparked and jagged
and bounced across my body,
through every limb and part,
but settled nowhere;
as a bird trapped in a room
veers and darts from one wall
to another, ceiling to floor.

Heat flared in my back:
a firework arching out
its tentacles – molten
ores and golden jets,
fading flakes of light
from earlier explosions,
a meteor shower sifting down
a black summer sky

– or a rose, wide
open, suddenly past
the crucial moment, letting
all its petals fall.
A thick, hot, blindingly
bright fluorescent tube
is pressed into my spine.
Then everything goes dark.

Jade

My toe won't heal,
for months needs dressing.
Maybe the cure is jade
with its gift of renewal,
a piece from the burial suit
of a Chinese emperor, which
he hoped would make him immortal.

Whole lives used
to quarry, slice, abrade
the precious stone
mottled green as a bruise,
a rare mouldy cheese,
into small rectangular plates
     like the counters and chips
     for a game no one alive
     can play, or the scaly
     back of a dragon-god
linked with gold wire
into a suit of armour
absurd and awesome
as a Lilliputian attempt
to gird Gulliver
or the determination
to survive aeons.

How long before a new
toenail grows from the root
to replace the damaged disk,
opaque as jade? What
did they see, what did they find,
that first moment when
the tomb was opened? Tarry
ochre-streaked remains and
the scattered, broken parts
of an empty suit.

IV

Signs and Wonders

Maps of million-year-long moments
when the poles reversed, the planet lurched,
shuddered, groaned and swung,

stripes of alternating magnetism
that show where molten rock, iron magma, rose
then flowed and still continues to spread

forever symmetrically outward
from mid-ocean ridges, core to surface,
script of a language no one yet can read

– or the perfect pattern of fingerprints,
clear marks left by the touch of whatever
unimaginable consciousness

will create and destroy with the same blind joy
new elements, continents and climates
forever. Its signs and wonders.

Spider Plant
(for Bertrand)

Is the spider plant an ordered or
chaotic system? Diagram
of bifurcation, binary network,
cascading complexity, it asks:
                    which path
will the energy take?

Like the aerial view of a river
augmented by shifting tributaries,
a wide slow delta altering
its palmate pattern, no way to know
where the next oscillation
                    will start,

which fine node on the pale stem
will swell and bud and open
a new growth of almost luminous
leaves – faintly striped tender
plasm, nor when
                    it will happen:

a further demonstration
of the random element, strange
attractors, act of God or
force of gravity: symmetry
                    perfected
into harmony.

Black Plastic and Poplars

The hard-edged clarity of plastic sheeting
stretched across a mound of winter fodder
weighted down by worn-out tractor tires.
Behind that super-realistic foreground
stands a fourteenth-century village church,
its yew tree sifting arrows and prisms –
watercolour of a vanished perspective.

Further into the picture a curving line
of poplars halfway up the hill – a northern
windbreak, vibrations of light and colour
against a cloudless, baby-blue sky. A lingering
autumn thins the foliage, spreads a deceptive
golden tinge of spring over the sharp tones,
the ammoniacal earthy stink of death,
bundled into black plastic bags.

Driving IV

A group of standing stones.
Men with hands stretched out
to touch each others' shoulders
blindly treading their slow dance
until the circle forms.

A twig studded with hard green buds
gripped by a blackbird's amber claws.
A clump of ivy thickening
a tree trunk to the shape of a body,
head slumped forward.

Four small planes in a hangar.
the dark propeller cones and gleam of
cockpit windows are the moist black snouts
and gentle eyes of four cows
watching from their stall.

Somerset August

A man stands silhouetted,
pondering his allotment,
against a flat horizon.
One hand rests on his spade,
the hip on the opposite side is raised
in the balanced diagonal slant
of a classical statue.

*

Arching from their banks, lianas
of brambles and tangles of nettle, hogweed,
wind flower and rosebay willowherb
darken the lane. It is still too soon
for their downy seeds to clog the hedge
like froth from a receding tide.

The trees have altered shape –
branches sunk, spread by the weight
of apples, hazelnuts and plums.
Across the valley, straight rows of maize,
with reddened tassels, could be vineyards.

Vague clouds, like milk dissolving in tea,
process from south to north – their shadows
dull the separate tones of the fields
then fade, and colours sharpen again.

*

A plane flew low and loud over the village
and flocks of birds bounced and whirled and swung
above the television aerials,
the pantiled roofs, the churchyard yew,
the breast-shaped hills –
then circled back.

Next year, everything will change.
No more cabbages or runner beans.
The windbreak of poplars behind him
will shelter scions and seedlings.
Now the children have left home,
he can grow flowers.

Autumn Crocus

Anomalous bright blossom
in late afternoon shadow.

Mercury-pale stems
surging out of the dark
earth: Halloween candles.

Mauve flowers with amber
yellow pollen-swollen anthers.

Each clump is bordered
by a halo of rotting
petals like votive objects
around a damaged ikon
or a martyr's statue.

Morpho

Blue like bolts of slubbed raw silk –
a fan unfolding flung across a counter
summer lightning coruscating
in the darkest corner
of a godown –
        like lapis, Persian enamel
        neon violet flashes
        from the deepest mica strata
        smeared rainbow prisms
        across the freeway's puddled asphalt
        a peacock's flaunt and shudder
        the burning sapphire antarctic heart

is the sky reflected
by the colourless transparent wings
        their pulsing beat
of a morpho butterfly
which moves through a haze of weightless scales
        like sequins loosened
        from a dancer's bodice sparking
        in the footlights' glare
        a yacht ringed by the foamy
        tarlatan skirt of its wake

to flare like a splutter of phosphorus
into the noonday zenith –
        ignite and vanish.

His Things

From the kitchen window
his wife watches
the old poet
stumble across
his windy garden

and well knows
that he pretends
such interest
in his frostburnt trees
their damaged bark
and seared foliage

to hide the tears
seeping down
his ashy cheeks'
unshaven stubble

his back to the house
and far enough
so she won't hear
him groan his grief
his rage and fear
of death aloud, as
he mourns his mother.

The Bench

(for Harry)

There used to be a wooden bench
under those trees –
this glade of chestnut, maple, flowering
thorn. It was more
than a decade ago, the day I sat there
after the call announcing your death.

Since then, the trees
have grown as much as trees will do
through several years.
Trunks have thickened, crowns of branches
spread and filled.
For months, I felt compelled to sit there
and think of you –
choosing the place, perhaps, in contrast
to the mood evoked, remembering.

The trees grew taller
the glade seemed darker, the bench collapsed.
But even now
the empty space vibrates with emotion
and I try to avoid it –
when I don't forget.

Those Trees

It must be the dawn chorus –
or are the birds that just woke me
perched on those trees:
my lost garden burgeoning beyond
the window, years receding
like scrims of painted scenery,
flimsy curtains drawn across
and closing off the street outside?

Those trees, here, are fuller
and taller than they were there and then.
Their branches are thicker, reach further now –
changed by how many years' growth?
Some part of my being stayed
with them, witnessing time
alter the shapes
of bushes and hedges, adding, subtracting,
substance and meaning. Are real birds
really singing this early, this winter
city morning – a dawn chorus –
or am I in that other house?
For they are more immediate
than memory: those trees.

Whatever It Was

I go to fetch something
but forget what it is
before I get there
    wherever that is
then go back again
two or three more times
before I remember

as a bird – is it a swallow?
circles darts and skims
round and down
across and up again
until the moment of contact
   to scoop
      out of the air
the spinning winged seed
the bright buzzing insect
the one glittering perfect object
– whatever it was.

Where and There and Here

Where did the mind swoop,
rapt and helpless, for what felt aeons
but it seems was only minutes?
(Time is different there.)

This has to be explained
in the language of science-fiction:
flashing stars and comets
scary, spongy blackness
the pulsing rhythm,
Superman & Wondergirl

teleported somewhere else,
another dimension, total transfer
toward that giddy angle of entry
which is the sense of return.

How long was I there,
absorbed and distracted,
where exactly was it?
(Though I know 'exactly' is a word
which doesn't belong –
any more than I do – here.)

The Gates

There is the labour of giving birth.
I have known that — at times even
remember the effort to be born.
Still to come is the work
of leaving life. I have seen how hard
it is for some, while others,
who one moment were present, the next
are gone. I have passed the gate
of flesh. Now, the wait — how long? —
to learn the final task, before
I am let through the gate of earth.

The Point of It All

Duplications and perspectives, like mirrored
halls or corridors in tourist hotels.
Static-sparking nylon carpets. Walls
a paler version of the same exhausted
colour under neon-strip illumination.
Smoothly-swinging double doors, marked
'Anarchy Storeroom', 'Betrayal Department'.
The usual anxiety dream
including it all.

This time, another actor on the scene:
someone I hoped might be the very ally
to help reduce the tension that oozed its poison
through weeping eyes and skin. Alone, I knew
how I would lose control at the worst moment
and foolishly encourage and confirm
the malice and pleasure of my tormentor
(now also present) – who had to be
the cause of it all.

Wearily, we quartered every corner,
exploring spaces musty as cupboards, huge
and drafty as shopping precincts – stumbled
across an empty office whose wide windows
opened on a sunset sky and showed how high
above the street we were. But it was always
the wrong place and time for easy answers.
The next part of the dream I forget:
the point of it all.

Poetry

I

Something reminds you of something else
of something that happened and what you felt
and then the memory reminds you
of something to make a comparison –

like the flight of birds which wheels and turns
here, today, against the clouds
outside the window like that web of birds
coordinated as a single creature

veering low to skim the poplars
and almost disappearing in
the noon dazzle – a farewell banner
flared across a brilliant sky –

above another garden for the last time
that last day. But even a memory
which only reminds you of something then doesn't
go further, might be the start of a poem.

II

A spider on its lengthening thread –
which I just noticed – is a reminder
of that still potent childish wish
to tug one end of a thick rope
passed through a pulley's grooved wheels
or an iron hook fixed high on the wall
of a bare whitewashed room (the other
end knotted around my neck),

to haul myself up like a sack of meal or
pannier of grapes, evade the limits
of matter's laws like a god who plays
at changing shape (stretched to a cord,
pressed spider-small, cut with the grain,
crushed with the grape): do the impossible –

while imagination, intoxicated,
veers through role, form, time and space
like a spider web's patterned versions
of what there is, what might be.

Its poetry.

V

Sugar-Paper Blue

I

Trying to describe a colour
by comparison and metaphor
is as futile as the attempt
to hum the tune I hear in my head.
But I thought everyone knew
what was meant by sugar-paper blue.

Sugar-paper – that thickish, stiffish
somewhat-grainy-surfaced, mottled
faded-navy paper glued or folded
into bags for sugar: the next image
is my aunt and mother sticky-fingered
in the family grocery store.

After school, pushing a metal scoop
through the shifting granular dampness
inside a hairy sack of jute,
they'd fill those bags, then do their homework.
        You understand, there is no proof
        this actually occurred.

I was trying to describe a room
in Leningrad (in '65
still the city's name), walls painted
the traditional nineteenth-century tone
I called sugar-paper blue,
to a friend in New York, years later.

II

It was the study of my guide's parents,
two polite Petersborgians
who had survived the siege,
their daughter said, with bodies gaunt
and eyes enormous as Rublev saints
on icons at the Hermitage ('That's
how we all looked'), and now, proudly,
showed books, albums, pamphlets
guarded through terrible years.

I turned the pages of thick or flimsy paper,
thought of those writers and artists
gone to the gulags or Paris, and knew
that I was touching holy relics.

'Here's Mandelstam's first published verse,' Galya
translated. 'These woodcuts are by Goncharova.
And look: Blok. Bely. Gumilev.'
'The Acmeist who married Akhmatova?'
(I was such a show-off.) 'Yes,' they confirmed.
'And this is the book with the cycle of poems
dedicated to her by Marina Tsvetaeva'
        – who titled them *The Muse*, and later said:
        'I read as if Akhmatova
        were the only person in the room.
        I read for the absent Akhmatova',
        – who didn't hear them, but carried the manuscript
        in her handbag for years, until
        it split at the folds and fell apart.

   III

I was probably not more than twelve when,
in my aunt's glass-fronted mahogany bookcase –
        dusting its elaborate clawed feet,
        the swagged garlands of leaves swathing
        the hips of the female torsos
        that surged from the column each side
        like naked caryatids, or
        twin figureheads with the fixed eyes
        and stern faces of implacable Fates
        on the vessel of expectation
        which that bookcase (the same piece now
        in my London apartment; the one object
        whose look and contents, I suspect,
        formed my taste in everything) became –
I found what can only be called
'a slim volume', with limp covers,
in an unknown script and language.

I don't remember Aunt Ann translating
one line from its pages, nor ever
explaining how she came to own it.
But she told me some facts about the woman
who wrote it – the first time I heard
those words: Anna Akhmatova –

  later, I wondered how important
  the coincidence of name might be for her,
  my aunt, who since the sugar-bagging days
  saw herself an artist-manqué;

  IV

'You are an admirer of Akhmatova?'
It was a loaded question, then.
Faces gleaming white against the dark
blue walls and shelves of books
as marble busts in a library,
all three watched me closely.

'You know I don't read Russian. But
there are a few translations – '
I couldn't go on. I felt ridiculous.
'She's ill now,' Galya said,
'but still in touch with everything.
And what a good neighbour.'

A neighbour? Hard to imagine her
in such a mundane situation.
Like the taut silk of a parachute
collapsing inward, billowed out,
by contrary winds, the barriers
of time and space changed shape and meaning.

'Do you hear that sound?' My gaze followed
Galya's to the ceiling. 'She must be
better today, she's walking around.'
'Anna Akhmatova lives upstairs?'
My awestruck, disbelieving voice
creaked like the floorboards.

V

Incredulous questions:
as if needing to hear the simple fact
reiterated yet again;
pleading that somehow they help me
to meet the famous poet,
the witness,
the sacred monster,
the old, dying woman –
                              or at least
        help me to see her –
        even if only over the shoulder
        of one of them – who could knock
        at her door and let me look
        even if only a moment –
        just to see her – a glimpse –
        Anna Akhmatova:
                              my obsessed
demand exceeded decent behaviour.
But they firmly insisted, repeating,
as many times as I asked, that what
I wanted could not happen.

VI

I have scanned encyclopaedias
and dictionaries, read every entry
under 'sugar' and 'paper' and 'blue':
endless, tedious searchings. But no one
acknowledges the relevance
of those qualifiers, or recognises
the description, though I see it
so clearly: a glaucous sheen
on the cheap, thick sheets of paper.
        Mandelstam – I hadn't read him
        then – might have written
        of sugar cones from North Africa,
        but eating blue grapes
        under 'the burning blue sky'
        of Tashkent, did Akhmatova notice
        one wrapped in blue paper?

(As for 'papier bleu', in *White Flock*
I found it: 'the blue copy-book
with the poems I wrote as a child'.)

There are other more poetic blues:
azure, cerulean, lapis lazuli,
ultramarine, cornflower, indigo;
(the colour of rivers and ocean,
the shadows on ice and snow).
But my imagination
stubbornly returns
to my aunt and mother,
Feigele and Channah – Fanny and Annie –
unhappily filling packets of sugar
(while sucking the crystal residue).
> It's not as if they came from Russia.
> Somewhere near Bukovina
> was where they were born.

Is it impossible to say:
standing side by side in the damp room
behind the store – like sisters
in a Dostoevsky novel –
their chilblained hands and feet
burned as blue with cold
as Anna Ahkmatova's
heart, mind, soul, body,

or allude to the janitor's blue cap,
or the blue lips
of the woman who whispered,
'Can you describe this?'
as she stood in line
three hundred hours
With the other mothers, wives and sisters
outside Kresty prison.
Is it shameful or shameless
that I can't disentangle the stories?
> How they all must have yearned
> for something to sweeten their mouths,
> or had they forgotten
> even the taste of sugar?

VII

Poetry, maternal figure. Sugar syrup, blue paper.

The Muse: a veiled girl with pipes in her hand.
Cassandra: '...my words prophesied those graves.'

    sugar syrup, blue paper

'Not quite a harlot, burning with passion;
not quite a nun, who can pray for forgiveness.'

    sugar syrup, blue paper

Orthodox Russian village women pilgrims.
Michal, Rachel, all the daughters of Israel.

    sugar syrup, blue paper

'They are very nice when they are courting.'
The face of a child with divorced parents.

    sugar syrup, blue paper

'Hiding her heart' from her husband,
drinking to 'loneliness spent together'.

    sugar syrup, blue paper

'Everyone looks through a foreign window.
One in Tashkent, another in New York.'

    Poetry.
    Maternal figure.
    Sugar syrup.
    Blue paper.

I wanted to see her.
I wanted to be initiated.
Like a hungry animal
wanting to push its muzzle
into the sticky, blue-sugar secrets
of suffering and poetry,
to lick the gritty essence of love
from the palm of her hand:
such were my ignorant, urgent demands.

The vibration of footsteps,
the sense of a body's bulk and weight
displacing space, the mystery
existing, alive and breathing
above my head, were maddening.

That was when – my first trip to Russia –
after letting me talk, and spin a rope
of hopeless platitudes more than
long enough to hang myself,
a stranger said: 'If you ever come back,
then I'll tell you how it really is.'

Glad to join our party – the table already
covered with half-empty bottles and glasses –
he then revealed he'd last seen his father
in the witness box at the Doctors' Plot trial.
Unsure if there would be a next visit,
his wife murmured, 'Murdered,' in my ear.

Remembering this, I had the childish wish
to take the misery of the century
compact it to a small black stone
with the density of a neutron star –
hundreds of million tons per cubic inch –
wrap it up in blue sugar-paper
then cast it into the core of a black hole
from which nothing can ever escape
from which the signals would come
dimmer and redder and fainter
until they stopped forever...

What I wanted would not happen. What
I wanted made the rest of my visit awkward.
Quite soon, Galya and I
were saying goodbye to her parents –
and that beautiful blue-papered study –
and walking down the stairs.
   The same stairs, etc. etc.
   All the obvious thoughts.

I stopped to look up at the grey façade
(a handsome building, as I recall) and,
thinking I was very cunning, casually asked,
'Which window is yours?' Half-reluctant,
half-amused, she gave the answer I hoped for.

There was a time,
in the forties, after the war,
when guards were posted
in the street outside her house,
and Anna Akhmatova
was obliged to appear,
morning and evening, at her window,
to confirm that she had not escaped
or killed herself.
     Though I stood
for a long time next day
on the opposite pavement
and stared at the window
hoping to see, behind
the spun-sugar lace of the curtain,
the pale blur of a face
which might be hers,
no one was there.

Sugar-Paper Blue

'a veiled girl...' As in Akhmatova's poem, *The Muse.*

'Cassandra' So Mandelstam had called Anna Akhmatova. In that 'persona', she wrote: 'Oh grief / my words prophesied those graves.'

'Not quite a harlot, etc...' From the critical essay about Akhmatova's work by G. Lelevich (1923).

'Michal, Rachel, all the daughters...' In the early 1920s, Akhmatova wrote about Old Testament heroines. She had already used the figure of the Orthodox village woman as a symbol of Russia, and of staunchness, etc.

'They are very nice...', 'Hiding her heart', 'loneliness spent together' Quoted from poems relating to Akhmatova's relationship with Nikolay Punin.

'child with divorced parents' Reference to Anna Akhmatova's son Lyova (Lev Nikolaevich Gumilev), her only child (by her first husband, the poet Nikolay Gumilev).

'Everyone looks through a foreign window...' Quoted from Akhmatova's *Poem without a Hero* (1940-1962).

Ruth Fainlight was born in New York City, and has lived mostly in England since the age of 15. Her father was born in London, and her mother in a small town on the eastern borders of the Austro-Hungarian Empire (now in Russia). She was educated at schools in America and England, and at Birmingham and Brighton colleges of art, and married the writer Alan Sillitoe in 1959. She was Poet in Residence at Vanderbilt University, Nashville, Tennessee, in 1985 and 1990, and received a Cholmondeley Award for Poetry in 1994. Ruth Fainlight lives in London.

Her many books include poetry, short stories, translations, drama and opera libretti. Her poems have appeared in numerous anthologies, and her stories in books including *Penguin Modern Stories 9* and *The Penguin Book of Modern Women's Stories* (1991).

Her poetry books include: *Cages* (1966) and *To See the Matter Clearly* (1968), from Macmillan in Britain and Dufour in the USA; *The Region's Violence* (1973), *Another Full Moon* (1976), *Sibyls and Others* (1980), *Fifteen to Infinity* (1983), *Selected Poems* (1987) and *The Knot* (1990), all from Hutchinson and Century Hutchinson; *This Time of Year* (1994) and *Selected Poems* (1995) from Sinclair-Stevenson; and *Climates* (1983) and *Sugar-Paper Blue* (1997) from Bloodaxe Books. *Fifteen to Infinity* was published in the USA by Carnegie Mellon University Press.

She has also translated two books of poetry from the Portuguese of Sophia de Mello Breyner, and collaborated with Alan Sillitoe on a translation of Lope de Vega's play *All Citizens Are Soldiers* (Macmillan, 1969). Her own poetry has been published in Portuguese (1995) and French (1997) editions.

She has published two collections of short stories, *Daylife and Nightlife* (André Deutsch, 1971) and *Dr Clock's Last Case* (Virago, 1994). Her libretti include: *The Dancer Hotoke* (1991), a chamber opera by Erika Fox (nominated for the Laurence Oliver Awards in 1992); *The European Story* (1993), a chamber opera by Geoffrey Alvarez; and *Bedlam Britannica* (1995), a *War Cries* TV opera directed by Celia Lowenstein with music by Robert Jan Stips.